TABLE OF CONTENTS

DISCLAIMER

This essay represents the views of the author and does not necessarily reflect the official opinion of the Air War College or the Department of the Air Force. In accordance with Air Force Regulation 110-8, it is not copyrighted, but is the property of the United States government.

Loan copies of this document may be obtained through the interlibrary loan desk of Air University Library, Maxwell Air Force Base, Alabama 36112-5564 (telephone [205] 953-7223 or DSN 493-7223).

ABSTRACT

TITLE: The Art of Intelligence

AUTHOR: Gary D. Payton, Colonel, USAF

Styled in the manner of Sun Tzu's classic, <u>The Art of War</u>, and set in the year 2017, the essay "The Art of Intelligence" describes principles and tenets inherent in intelligence. Not bounded by time or changing technology, the principles of *accuracy, timeliness, usability, fusion, relevancy, intellectual honesty,* and the requirement to be *communicated,* combine with the tenets of *politics, timing,* and the *multilevel* nature of military operations to form the basics of the art. If understood by the intelligence professional and the commander, the application of the intelligence principles and tenets can greatly enhance the conduct of military operations at the strategic, operational, and tactical levels.

BIOGRAPHICAL SKETCH

Colonel Gary D. Payton (B.S., USAF Academy; M.A.S., Johns Hopkins University; and, M.A., Georgetown University) has served in a wide variety of command and staff positions as an intelligence officer. His assignments range from squadron level, to major command, to defense agency both in the United States (Alaska, Hawaii, Maryland, and Texas) and abroad (Germany, Turkey, and the United Kingdom). During the Persian Gulf War, he commanded an RC-135/RIVET JOINT squadron providing tactical intelligence support to coalition forces in Operations Proven Force and Provide Comfort. He is a graduate of the Squadron Officers School, the Air Command and Staff College, and the Air War College, class of 1993. Colonel Payton has previously published in the Air University Journal, Military Review, Journal of Modern African Studies, and Checkpoints, the magazine of the Air Force Academy Association of Graduates.

PREFACE

*Now the reason the enlightened prince and the
wise general conquer the enemy whenever they move
and their achievements surpass those of ordinary
men is foreknowledge.*

-*Sun Tzu*

The essay "The Art of Intelligence" is the "final product"
of a future Deputy Chief for Staff for Intelligence, United
States Air Force. The author, an unnamed General, enjoyed an
almost 30 year career as an intelligence officer spanning 1987
to the spring of 2017. Faced with the impact of the information
explosion on the quantity of "raw data" available to
intelligence professionals, he undertook a project to distill
intelligence to its very essence. The principles and tenets
described here form the fundamental truths of the art.

Styled in the manner of Sun Tzu's classic, <u>The Art of War</u>,
as edited by Samuel B. Griffith and using the same technique of
assertion and expert commentary, this essay describes the
principles and tenets of intelligence which are universal across
time and stand the test of changing technology.

BIOGRAPHY OF THE GENERAL

*The ultimate objective of intelligence is to
enable action to be optimized.*
- Dr R. V. Jones
Chief, British Scientific Intelligence
World War II

The General died Monday while TDY to San Antonio. His last
day in the Pentagon was like hundreds of others - quick reviews
of intelligence background papers for the Chief, planning for the
upcoming Senior Intelligence Officers' Conference, telephone
calls regarding the placement of Colonels in key positions around
the Air Force. Late Friday after he stuffed the last few folders
in his briefcase and turned to leave the office, he flipped the
keys of his locked desk to his executive officer. "Just in
case!" the General called. "Just in case," replied the exec as
he caught the keys and dropped them into his desk. It was a
departure ritual they had carried out countless times. This time
was the last time.

He had been the best of a new breed of intelligence
officers - a "generalist" skilled in intelligence operations and
intelligence application. Unlike the many Deputy and Assistant
Chiefs of Staff for Intelligence before him, he had not
progressed in a "stovepiped" discipline of Signals Intelligence,
Imagery Intelligence, or Human Resources Intelligence. Rather,
the career path he followed had been envisioned by Senior
Intelligence Officers in the 1980s and codified by the major

1

changes to Air Force Specialty Codes in the early 1990s.(39:3)

Across a series of assignments that included wartime duty with a F-111 fighter wing, leadership at a major Signals Intelligence collection site, and joint duty on the Unified Command staff at US Strategic Command, the General watched and learned how intelligence supported - or failed to support - military commanders.

His Desert Storm experience with the 48th Tactical Fighter Wing in Saudi Arabia anchored his entire career. As a junior officer, he devoted months at RAF Lakenheath in England to gaining the confidence of the pilots and weapons systems officers who flew the venerable Aardvark.(20:--) During the pre-war buildup, he and his enlisted intelligence specialists honed their skills in building target folders, briefing and debriefing crews, and providing his Wing Commander with comprehensive intelligence reports on Saddam Hussein's forces. But when the air war began, nothing he could do at the unit level could get post-strike satellite imagery of the military targets into their hands fast enough. Their appetite for imagery was insatiable and could not be met.(17:338) Despite the many successes of intelligence in Desert Storm, a generation of future Air Force leaders convinced themselves that intelligence failed because they as pilots were unable to get timely pictures of their strike missions.

In the 1970s and 1980s when an intelligence officer was characterized by the nature of his or her technical training (for example being viewed as a SIGINTer, a Photo Interpreter, or a

HUMINTer), the opportunity to lead large numbers of Air Force people was not equally available to junior intelligence officers. When career emphasis and training shifted to being a "generalist," officers like himself began to receive assignments to key positions across a wide range of Major Commands based on their leadership skills and managerial ability, not just on their past affiliation with a technical specialty. The General's future was shaped by the breaking down of these historic barriers.

As a captain, he served as a flight commander at one of the Air Force Intelligence Agency's most important overseas field sites, the 6903rd Electronic Security Group at Osan Air Base, Korea. He was thrust into the role of leading over 40 specialists in their around-the-clock role of providing vital intelligence support to the Commander, Seventh Air Force, and to the US and South Korean chain-of-command.

"Up close and personal" characterized the General's leadership opportunity in Korea. He led his flight by personal example. He motivated. He delegated. He empowered. He disciplined. His daily activities ranged from team building and goal setting through working the dozens of personal problems his subordinates brought to him caused by a year's separation from family in the States. And, most importantly, along the way he absorbed the myriad of details associated with high tech intelligence collection. He learned the strengths, and he learned the weaknesses, and he began to ponder the enduring principles and tenets of intelligence in support of military operations.

Years later as the US Strategic Command Director of Intelligence, or J-2, the General served in Omaha as a principal advisor to his four-star Commander in Chief on such critical issues as START III and global weapons of mass destruction. He recognized clearly the political impact of his counsel when his military views on treaty compliance clashed with those of the Department of State or the Central Intelligence Agency. He saw first hand how timely and accurate intelligence shaped policy on issues vital to the security of the United States.

For nearly three decades, the General served as an intelligence officer. From the aircraft shelters of Saudi Arabia to the halls of the Pentagon, he helped shape intelligence products delivered to commanders. From "bombs on target" to national security decision making, he understood the value of piercing the enemy's secrets while protecting one's own.(34:185)

It wasn't until Thursday, after the majority of the details for the Arlington Cemetery funeral were ironed out, that the General's executive officer opened the locked desk. Patiently, the exec separated personal items from official documents and classified messages. In the bottom drawer in a hanging folder marked "Art" and bulging with dozens of yellow highlighted and annotated articles and clippings, he found the draft manuscript and the illustrative comments the General had asked his closest confidants to prepare on each major subject.

Excerpts of this final product of the General, "The Art of Intelligence," were first published four months after his death.

PRINCIPLES

*Intelligence is an instrument of conflict.
It consists of words, numbers, images, suggestions,
appraisals, incitements. It consists also of
truths that enlighten or mislead, or of outright
falsehoods. Because it is immaterial, intelligence
cannot wound. But its use has led to the killing
or saving of millions.*
                                        -Angelo Codevilla

The General said:

Accuracy

1. *Accuracy* is the prime principle of military intelligence.
With accurate intelligence, all aspects of strategic,
operational, and tactical planning and execution proceed on the
basis of fact. Without accurate intelligence on the enemy's
location, capability, and intent, planning is an unfocused and
wasteful exercise and execution may result in defeat.

2. Accurate intelligence is a necessary condition for victory.
It is not, however, a sufficient condition to gain the victory.
Intelligence does not pilot air and space vehicles, nor field
armies, nor sail ships at sea. Intelligence instead supports the
maneuver, the surprise, the security, and the economy of combat
forces to achieve their objective.

The Historian: Accurate intelligence serves as a powerful
force enhancer. In the largest single air battle of the second
half of the twentieth century, the Israeli Air Force (IAF)
devastated the Syrian Air Force on 9 June 1982. To support

"Operation Peace for Galilee," the IAF's mission was to neutralize Syrian SA-6 sites and destroy reacting enemy fighters. At every juncture, planning and execution was enhanced by accurate intelligence. In the one year period following the April 1981 introduction of SA-6 missiles into the Beka'a Valley, Israeli military intelligence focused on the new surface-to-air threat. Their successes allowed aircrews to rehearse the strike missions in the Negev desert against highly accurate replicas of the missile sites. On the day of the attack, superb tactical intelligence contributed to success. Syrian airspace was scanned by E-2C surveillance aircraft flying off the Lebanese coast. A Boeing 707 signals intelligence platform monitored Syrian communications and radar activity. With F-15 and F-16 pilots flying combat air patrols, IAF F-4s armed with Shrike, Standard ARM, and Maverick missiles, and F-16s loaded with standoff weapons and conventional munitions attacked nineteen SA-6 sites and several SA-2 and SA-3 sites. In a superb example of real-time intelligence application, the IAF strike commander monitored the on-going operation from video provided by forward orbiting Scout and Mastiff RPVs. On the first day of the air campaign, 17 SA-6 sites were destroyed along with several SA-2 and SA-3 installations. On 9 June, the Israelis downed 23 Syrian MiG-21s and MiG-23s. On 10 June, they shot down 15 more. By the end of September, Israeli pilots had destroyed 29 SAM sites in seven raids, 85 Syrian MiGs, and lost only two IAF

aircraft to enemy ground fire.(29:128-133) Accurate intelligence
contributed mightily to this successful air campaign.

The General said:

Timeliness

3. Victory in battle is gained by the side which operates at the
faster tempo or rhythm. The *timeliness* of intelligence
contributes directly to the commander's ability to observe,
orient, decide, and act. With timely intelligence, the commander
is able to act at a faster tempo, generate confusion and disorder
in the adversary, and achieve victory. Without timely
intelligence, the commander's observation and orientation is
delayed. His decisions and actions, therefore, are slower and
initiative and leverage are lost to the enemy.(6:--)

The Engineer: The delivery of ever more timely intelligence
was a central focus of the intelligence engineering community in
the two decades following the 1991 Persian Gulf War. Our initial
combat successes following Desert Storm were based on collocating
the intelligence collection and communications assets of the Air
Force Intelligence Agency (AFIA) with the air operations center
of the Air Combat Command forces.(5:16) When the 366th Wing at
Mountain Home AFB, Idaho, deployed to Tunisia in 1995 in response
to the Libyan incursion, AFIA's specialists worked side-by-side
with the Wing's own intelligence and planning staff. With an

8

organic collection capability and on-line access to national
intelligence networks, timely intelligence kept the commander's
decisions and actions inside the Libyan's own decision cycle.
Our greatest successes, though, flowed from the engineering
breakthroughs at the turn of the century. When we solved the
data compaction problem of the multispectral imaging satellites,
we could at last take full advantage of Virtual
Reality (VR).(27:43-46) It had all come together before the
Iranian military launched the Second Gulf War in 2010.(18:11)
Timely intelligence produced a dramatic impact on operational
planning and tactical execution. In the battle cab at the Air
Operations Center in Dhahran, Saudi Arabia, the Joint Force Air
Component Commander (JFACC) swivelled into a VR depiction of his
next day's Air Tasking Order. The image generators driven by a
direct digitized satellite feed produced a detailed, three-
dimensional image of the air campaign. By selecting the
appropriate icons, the commander viewed Iranian air defenses,
advancing divisions, and ballistic missile trajectories. He then
overlaid the friendly air attacks accelerated in time.

Yet even with seeing his own air forces move across the
border to attack Iranian targets, Virtual Reality allowed him to
move in space and produce a "God's eye" view of how his incoming
air and missile attack looked from the Iranian commander's
perspective.(8:58) Not only did timely intelligence aid his
observation and orientation by creating a telepresence of our
attack from the Iranian viewpoint, the JFACC could "get inside

9

the mind" of his opposing commander.(33:20)

Results at the squadron level were equally impressive. The Virtual Reality Advanced Planning System was near-real-time threat based. The imagery intelligence and signals intelligence feed was linked with weather information and merged with the mapping database. In short, aircrews could mission plan, rehearse, and select weapons employment alternatives based on intelligence data collected just minutes prior to takeoff.(21:38-41) Timely intelligence successfully contributed to an even faster decision-making tempo. Sustained across the first weeks of the campaign, the tempo forced the Iranian offensive to collapse into itself.(6:--) The remaining leaders in Teheran complied with all coalition demands for conflict termination.

The General said:

Usability

4. Intelligence must be usable to have value. If it is not tailored to meet the needs of the commander, intelligence has no *usability* and makes no contribution to military planning and execution.

5. Intelligence is a product. Users of intelligence are customers. If the product delivered to the customer is unusable, then the customer's intelligence needs go unsatisfied, and the

production costs of creating the product are wasted.

6. Making intelligence usable is a part of effective marketing. First, determine what the customer wants and needs. Wants and needs are not often identical. Second, tailor the intelligence production process to create the agreed upon product. Third, deliver an accurate and timely product in a usable format. Four, ask the customer for feedback on the product's usability. Five, absorb the feedback and begin again.

The Executive Officer: I first worked for the General in Omaha. He was a brutal editor, or that's what his intelligence analysts and middle managers first thought. In fact, his harsh editorial comments were consistently aimed at making the array of intelligence products more usable to the customer. He developed this simple "Usability Checklist:"

1. Does this intelligence product meet the customer's needs? How do you know? How do you know you know?
2. Does it answer the question asked?
3. Is the main point "up front?"
4. Is it as concise as you can get it?

Across the spectrum of intelligence products, the General sought to make them usable to the customer. Does the draft National Intelligence Estimate provide a focused analysis of the issue so the National Security Council can develop a new policy option? Does the enemy weapon's estimate produced for the USAF research and development community have sufficient detail to plan the Air Force's next generation system? Does the current intelligence briefing provide unique insights or information to aid the commander in deciding on a course of action? Is the myriad of electronic order of battle information delivered in a usable format to the mission planner, the electronic warfare officer, or the pilot? Is the threat data streaming into the cockpit of the orbiting F-22 usable in aiding the pilot to conduct her defensive counter air mission?

A trivial example illustrates the principle of usability. The General shocked his Pentagon intelligence staff the day he directed that all written replies to the Chief's questions would be limited to two data screens or one printed page. He hammered the point. The customer needed concise, to-the-point replies directly answering the question. No room to showcase personal knowledge of air and space power in the 21st century. No room to provide flowing prose amplifications of supporting data. Understand the need. Answer directly. Get the main point "up front." Be concise and be done.

The General said:

Fusion

7. Fused intelligence is a finished intelligence product produced from more than one source of intelligence information. *Fusion* draws upon the complementary strengths of Signals

Intelligence (what they said or what their radars emanated),
Imagery Intelligence (what it looks like), Human Intelligence
(information derived from a human source revealed through overt
or covert collection).

8. Fused intelligence creates the most accurate and complete
picture of what is known about an activity. In the absence of
fused intelligence, products are one-dimensional. While the
level of detail in single-source reports may be sufficient to
meet narrowly defined customer needs, fused reports are essential
to gain an in-depth understanding.

9. Because the enemy will try to deceive you, guard against
placing unquestioned trust in a single-source intelligence
report. What you hear, what you see, or what you are told may be
a lie or a fabrication. It is far more difficult to be deceived
when you rely on fused intelligence.

The Historian: On 1 January 1945, the Luftwaffe conducted a
highly successful attack against allied aircraft located on
liberated Belgium airfields. In a post-attack assessment, the
intelligence staff of the 12th Army Group Headquarters realized
they had received adequate SIGINT and HUMINT reporting to have
provided tactical warning to the commander. The reports,
however, were not fused. Highly compartmented ULTRA intercepts
received before the German attack indicated Operation Goldregen

13

was being launched. The SIGINT specialist had no knowledge from his source of an Operation Goldregen. Filed elsewhere in the headquarters, a POW interrogation report (an aspect of HUMINT) of a former Luftwaffe clerk in Berlin described aspects of Operation Goldregen - a plan to employ low flying aircraft in large numbers. No fusion. Extensive compartmentalization. Single-source intelligence information held within "stove piped" structures. Airmen died. Aircraft were destroyed.(31:24)

The General said:

Relevancy

10. Intelligence has *relevancy* if it contributes to the commander's ability to execute his mission at his level of military operation. No matter how accurate, timely, or fused the intelligence is, if it is not germane to the commander's needs it could detract from overall mission accomplishment.

11. What is highly relevant intelligence at one level of military activity, may be of limited relevance at another level. Intelligence production, therefore, must be geared to meet the distinctive needs of commanders across the full spectrum of military operations.

The Wing Commander: As the wartime commander of an F-125 fighter-bomber wing, I faced similar challenges in the Second

Gulf War that my predecessors faced in 1991. Intelligence must be relevant to the mission it supports. If the intelligence lacks relevancy, it extracts a price in time required to read it, watch it, or be briefed on it. Twenty years ago, field commanders criticized much of the Desert Storm intelligence as being designed for high-level policy-makers. It was too general, too broad-gaged. Much of what they got at the wing, division and brigade level wasn't relevant to mission planning and execution.(17:340-342)

At my level, I wanted to know about Iranian targets. When your mission is to kill road-mobile Khomeini intermediate range ballistic missiles at night, intelligence on camouflage and concealment techniques, dummy launchers, reload and refire capability, and relocation schemes is what's needed. Incoming reporting, therefore, on international political developments and domestic reactions in foreign capitals is not my idea of relevant intelligence. Don't get me wrong, I understand the value of such intelligence at other levels. But when you're in the thick of it, if intelligence isn't contributing to putting ordnance on target, then I don't want to hear it!

Consider what my Wing's intelligence needs were when the senior Iranian military leadership relocated to the Shiite religious center of Qom. Nondestructive or "disabling" munitions were the only option to drive them out.(16:45) High explosives, even from our best precision guided munitions, were absolutely out of the question. The task, then, was to shut down the entire

15

electrical grid in the city. You've heard the old adage, "Precision weapons need precision intelligence."(8:53) We needed it. We got it. And, it was relevant. Precise coordinates for every power station and substation serving the city. Detailed engineering reports from the Japanese contractors who built the transformers. Satellite imagery that drove the image generator in our Visual Reality Advanced Planning System. We got it all. Then, we planned the mission, rehearsed it in VR, and executed. We completely "put their lights out!" With relevant and precise intelligence contributing to mission success, the Iranian generals were driven out of the sanctuary of Qom and back to Teheran.

The General said:

Intellectual Honesty

12. *Intellectual honesty* must be a cardinal element in intelligence reporting. Accuracy and honesty are not the same. Accuracy is the absence of factual mistakes or errors. Honesty, however, is the adherence to facts and the truthfulness with which those facts are interpreted and presented.

13. Moral courage is required to remain intellectually honest and to resist the pressure to reach intelligence "conclusions" which are not supported by facts. The same moral courage and intellectual honesty must extend to reporting even what you do

16

not know, no matter how unpleasant that may be in the short term.

14.   Intellectual honesty must drive the intelligence professional to distinguish for the commander those conclusions which are solidly grounded in fact and those which are extrapolations or extensions of the fact. The commander cannot be left with uncertainty in his mind regarding what is fact, what is an estimate, and what is opinion.

The Mentor: My colleagues at the Agency always knew I was an Air Force intelligence analyst in the Pentagon of the 1970s. Occasionally, one of them who had studied the record would ask, "Was the Air Force estimate that the Soviet Backfire bomber had intercontinental capability intellectually honest?" I have concluded over the years that the answer to the question must be "no." Let me explain.

When the new supersonic bomber appeared at the Kazan aircraft plant in 1969, it validated the long-held Air Force prediction of a new Soviet bomber. In 1971, the aircraft, now designated the Backfire, was noted in aerial refueling from a tanker near the test center of Ramenskoye, just east of Moscow. The mission of the bomber, peripheral attack or intercontinental attack, now became one of the most fiercely contested intelligence debates of the Cold War. The predominant view of the Washington intelligence community was that the Backfire was a peripheral attack weapon and would not play a significant role in a strategic air attack on the United States. Supporting this position was the Backfire's limited payload, modest self-defense capabilities, and anticipated difficulty in staging the aircraft from far northern Siberian bases.(30:257-268) The Air Force strongly dissented and consistently argued the Backfire *could* be used for intercontinental attack - even if the aircraft flew one-way missions.(12:424) The key variable was the estimate of the range of the aircraft. A series of competitive analyses to determine the range produced dissimilar results and failed to conclusively end the debate.(15:85-86)

In short, though we lacked hard evidence that the Soviet Long Range Aviation Backfires ever rehearsed intercontinental strikes, the Air Force estimate of range and intent drove our institutional position that it could and would be used in an attack on the United States.(9:24)

The most troublesome aspect about the "intellectual honesty" of our intelligence estimate was the connection between the threat estimate and Air Force hardware procurement. At the time, the Air Force was fighting for the B-1 as a replacement for the aging B-52. F-15 fighter production was expanding to produce large numbers of highly capable air-to-air fighters.

There is an ethical difference between "worst case analysis" of the threat and the prudent planning and procurement which flows from the analysis and the deliberate overstatement of the threat to drive budget increases for expanded weapons buys. In the first case, intelligence serves to warn the nation's leaders

18

in sufficient time to respond deliberately. In the second case, intelligence is prostituted to the goal of "buying more metal." While the end result may be the same, one end is derived at honestly and the other dishonestly.

The General said:

Communicated

15. The power of intelligence to aid the commander in planning and executing military missions is nothing if the intelligence is not *communicated*. To know the enemy's intent, capabilities, and location has no worth until the commander receives, understands, and acts upon the intelligence.

16. It is the responsibility of the intelligence professional to choose the most effective way to inform the commander. To choose the spoken word, the written word, the picture, or the map is a critical decision. Only by knowing well the commander whom he or she serves, can the intelligence officer choose wisely.

The Teacher: If my students fail to communicate, they fail to serve. Behind the delivery of an accurate and timely intelligence product is a vast, multibillion dollar structure designed to manage, collect, process, and analyze information. Yet, the decades of technological and human investment are wasted if the intelligence officer can not communicate.

In the schoolhouse, I teach my students to think critically. I teach them to write with precision. I teach them to brief with clarity and conciseness. When the teaching stops it is their responsibility to learn and to do. To do well is to communicate.

The intelligence officers who most effectively serve their commanders develop a *persona*. Some are scholars. Some are showman. Some take on the outward appearances of the commander they serve. The particular *persona* that develops is irrelevant. What is important is if the style they adopt helps them communicate the intelligence.

When they engage the mind of the one they serve, they can successfully influence the formulation of a policy, plan, or the execution of a dangerous mission. They can be an aid to victory and a contributor to saving lives. If they fail to communicate the intelligence well, the commander will continue toward the objective, but without the full power of foreknowledge.

AFTERWARD

> *What is called "foreknowledge" cannot be elicited from spirits, nor from gods, nor by analogy with past events, nor from calculations. It must be obtained from men who know the enemy situation.*
> — *Sun Tzu*

The General said:

Intelligence is art and not science because it is a creation of people not nature. People collect intelligence. People analyze intelligence. People make human judgments as an intelligence product is created. And, ultimately, a person communicates the intelligence to the commander.

Thusfar, I have described the principles of intelligence as the fundamental truths of the art. *Accuracy, timeliness, usability, fusion, relevancy, intellectual honesty,* and the requirement to be *communicated* are all principles inherent in intelligence and are not bounded by time or changing technology. While these principles form the basics of the art, they are complemented by the supporting tenets of *politics, timing,* and the *multilevel* nature of military operations. These tenets further characterize intelligence as art.

Intelligence is a political process. It involves the judicious relay of intelligence from a person to a commander who is empowered to act upon the intelligence. It involves interaction between groups of people who represent powerful institutions. Typically, these interactions are between intelligence professionals and operations professionals. And, ultimately, the success of the intelligence process may rest on the personal relationship developed over time between the intelligence officer and the commander whom he serves. To work best, this relationship must involve trust, mutual respect, and a shared dedication to the mission.

To have the greatest impact on the commander, the *timing* of the delivery of the intelligence is crucial. The principle of timeliness and the tenet of timing are not the same. Timing involves the calculation of when to present the intelligence to the commander. If the timing is wrong and the commander is unable to focus on the intelligence, the impact of the information delivered may be diminished. It is the responsibility of the intelligence officer to pick the best timing for the delivery of the most important intelligence.

Finally, intelligence has a *multilevel* character as it supports missions at the tactical, operational, or strategic levels of warfare.(22:27) When supporting tactical operations, intelligence is highly perishable. The usability of the information may be measured in hours, minutes, and increasingly in seconds. Should intelligence fail, the impact, while deadly and locally dramatic, can be offset with other local victories. At the operational or theater level, intelligence has a lengthier period of usability. With an emphasis on enemy force disposition and capability, the gravity of operational intelligence greatly exceeds that of the tactical level. Should major intelligence errors occur, the impact on the theater campaign may be disastrous and not recoverable. At the strategic level, intelligence supporting national security decision making has a much longer usability. Likewise, it must reflect the political, economic, as well as military characteristics of the adversary nation. At this highest level, the consequences of misestimating are nationally profound.

Intelligence, then, is art created by people. And, the impact of that art on the decisions of the commander is greater than that of any other input he receives. Indeed, the "words, numbers, images, suggestions, appraisals, (and) incitements" describe the enemy and help the commander "optimize" his action to accomplish the mission. And, in the victory that follows the commander can claim he was served well by the art of intelligence.

Washington D.C.
19 April 2017

BIBLIOGRAPHY

1. Air Force Manual (AFM) 1-1. "Basic Aerospace Doctrine of the
   United States Air Force." 16 March 1984.

2. Air Force Manual (AFM) 1-1. "Basis Aerospace Doctrine of the
   United States Air Force, Vol. 1." March 1992.

3. Air Force Manual (AFM) 3-I (Draft). "Air Force Functional
   Doctrine: Aerospace Intelligence Doctrine." May 1992.

4. Andrews, Duane P. Memorandum on "Intelligence Support to
   Military Operations." U.S. Department of Defense
   Assistant Secretary of Defense for Command, Control,
   Communications, and Intelligence, 20 August 1992,
   Washington, D.C.

5. Bird, Julie. "Battle Planned Without Middleman." Air Force
   Times, 29 March 1993, p. 16.

6. Boyd, John R. "A Discourse on Winning and Losing." Seminar
   conducted at the Air War College, Maxwell AFB, Alabama,
   6-8 April 1993.

7. Burke, Gerard K. "Backfire: Strategic Implications."
   Military Review, September 1976, pp. 85-90.

8. Campen, Alan D. "Communications Support to Intelligence." In
   The First Information War, pp. 51- 60. Edited by Alan D.
   Campen. Fairfax, Virginia: AFCEA International Press,
   1992.

9. "Cassandra of the Cold War." Newsweek, 10 January 1977,
   p. 24.

10. Clapper, James R., Jr. "Desert War: Crucible for
    Intelligence Systems." In The First Information War,
    pp. 81-85. Edited by Alan D. Campen. Fairfax, Virginia:
    AFCEA International Press, 1992.

11. Colby, William E. "Tactical Intelligence: The Need for
    Improvement." Defense Intelligence Journal, Spring 1992,
    pp. 75-80.

12. Colby, William E. Honorable Men: My Life in the CIA. New
    York: Simon and Schuster, 1978.

13. Coyne, James P. Airpower in the Gulf. Arlington, Virginia:
    Air Force Association, 1992.

14. Culbertson, Charles N. "Air Intelligence and the Search for the Center of Gravity." Air War College Research Report, Air University, 1988.

15. Day, Bonner. "Soviet Bombers: A Growing Threat." _Air Force Magazine_, November 1978, pp. 84-87.

16. Debban, Alan W. "Disabling Systems: War-Fighting Option for the Future." _Airpower Journal_, Spring 1993, pp. 44-50.

17. Department of Defense. _Conduct of the Persian Gulf Conflict: An Interim Report to Congress_. Washington, DC: Government Printing Office, 1991.

18. Dunlap, Charles J., Jr. "The Origins of the American Military Coup of 2021." _Parameters_, Winter 1992-1993, pp. 2-20.

19. Futrell, Robert F. "U.S. Army Air Forces Intelligence in the Second World War." In _The Conduct of the Air War in the Second World War_, pp. 527-552. Edited by Horst Boog. Oxford, UK: Berg Publishers Limited, 1992.

20. Gibson, Susan B. Chief of Intelligence, 48th Tactical Fighter Wing, RAF Lakenheath, United Kingdom, 1988-1991. Interview, 4 April 1993.

21. Griffin, Louisa. "U.S. Mission Planning Systems Strive For Portability." _Defense Electronics_, February 1992, pp. 38-41.

22. Handel, Michael I. "Intelligence and Military Operations." In _Intelligence and Military Operations_, pp. 1- 69. Edited by Michael I. Handel. London: Frank Cass and Company Limited, 1990.

23. Handel, Michael I. _Sun Tzu and Clausewitz: The Art of War and On War Compared_. Carlisle Barracks, Pennsylvania: Strategic Studies Institute, US Army War College, 1991.

24. Handel, Michael I. _War, Strategy and Intelligence_. London: Frank Cass and Company Limited, 1989.

25. Holman, G. Paul, Jr. "Estimative Intelligence." In _The Military Intelligence Community_, pp. 129- 143. Edited by Gerald W. Hopple and Bruce W. Watson. Boulder, Colorado: Westview Press, 1986.

26. Hopkins, Robert S., III. "Ears of the Storm." In _The First Information War_, pp. 65-70. Edited by Alan D. Campen. Fairfax, Virginia: AFCEA International Press, 1992.

27. Jenish, D'arcy. "Fantastic Voyages." Maclean's, 14 December
        1992, pp. 42-46.

28. Jermano, Jill L. and Springer, Susan D. "Monitoring Road-
        Mobile Missiles Under START: Lessons from the Gulf War."
        Parameters, Spring 1993, pp. 70-80.

29. Lambeth, Benjamin S. "Moscow's Lessons from the 1982 Lebanon
        Air War." In War in the Third Dimension, pp. 127-148.
        Edited by R. A. Mason. London: Brassey's Defence
        Publishers, 1986.

30. Prados, John. The Soviet Estimate: U.S. Intelligence
        Analysis & Soviet Strategic Forces. Princeton, New
        Jersey: Princetown University Press, 1986.

31. Project RAND Report. "Notes on Strategic Air Intelligence in
        World War II (ETO)." October 1949. Quoted in Charles N.
        Culbertson, "Air Intelligence and the Search for the
        Center of Gravity," p. 24. Air War College Research
        Report, Air University, 1988.

32. Romm, Joseph J. "The Gospel According to Sun Tzu." Forbes,
        9 December 1991, pp. 154-162.

33. Safire, William. "Virtual Reality." New York Times Magazine,
        13 September 1992, pp. 18-20.

34. Seabury, Paul, and Codevilla, Angelo. War: Ends and Means.
        New York: Basic Books, Inc., 1989.

35. Soyster, Harry E. "Extending Real-Time Intelligence to
        Theater Level." In The First Information War, pp. 61-64.
        Edited by Alan D. Campen. Fairfax, Virginia: AFCEA
        International Press, 1992.

36. Sun Tzu. The Art of War. Translated by Samuel B. Griffith.
        London: Oxford University Press, 1963.

37. Swenson, Russell G. "The Warning and Crisis Support Functions
        in Regional Joint Intelligence Centers." Defense
        Intelligence Journal, Spring 1992, pp. 81-93.

38. "The Fight To Change How America Fights." U.S. News & World
        Report, 6 May 1991, pp. 30-31.

39. West, Joe. "Specialty Codes To Be Renumbered November 1."
        Air Force Times, 29 March 1993, p. 3.